FRENCH
FRIES

Thank you, Katja, our Queen of Sauces, without you french fries would merely be salted.

This cook book was composed to the best of our knowledge and belief. Neither the publisher nor the authors bear responsibility for unwanted reactions or adverse effects, which arise from processing of ingredients.

The authors thank the Ritzenhoff & Breker company for their kind support.

Copyright © 2015 by Schiffer Publishing Ltd.

Library of Congress Control Number: 2015949077

Originally published as Pommes Frites Internationale Rezepte, Dips & Tricks by Heel, Konigswinter, © 2013, Heel Verlag GmbH

Translated from the German by Omicron Language Solutions.

Type set in The Serif, Old Press & Chalkduster

ISBN: 978-0-7643-4965-2
Printed in China

Published by Schiffer Publishing, Ltd.
4880 Lower Valley Road
Atglen, PA 19310
Phone: (610) 593-1777; Fax: (610) 593-2002
E-mail: Info@schifferbooks.com

For our complete selection of fine books on this and related subjects, please visit our website at www.schifferbooks.com. You may also write for a free catalog.

This book may be purchased from the publisher. Please try your bookstore first.

We are always looking for people to write books on new and related subjects. If you have an idea for a book, please contact us at proposals@schifferbooks.com.

Schiffer Publishing's titles are available at special discounts for bulk purchases for sales promotions or premiums. Special editions, including personalized covers, corporate imprints, and excerpts can be created in large quantities for special needs. For more information, contact the publisher.

CHRISTINE HAGER · ULRIKE REIHN

FRENCH FRIES

International Recipes,

Dips & Tricks

4880 Lower Valley Road • Atglen, PA 19310

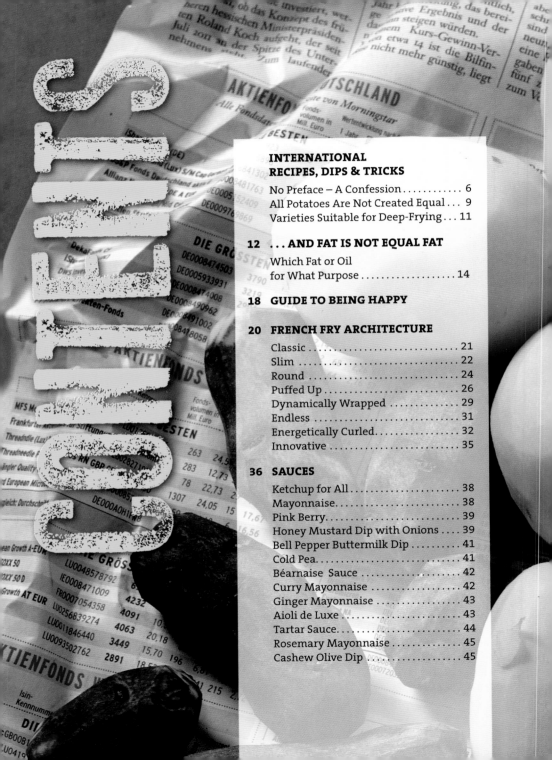

CONTENTS

NO PREFACE—
A CONFESSION

Actually, we should be grateful. Nothing else. Grateful for one of the most amazing discoveries of humankind. And yet, we feel a bit of envy, when we look at our western neighbors. Not because of the notorious patience with which the Belgians tolerate the potholes in their highways. No, they invented french fries, and succeeded in practically turning the twice-fried potato sticks into a synonym for Belgium. As inseparable from the nation as Nuremberg brats from the Franconian metropolis, pig's stomach from the Palatinate, and pork roast from Bavaria. However, very few German culinary manifests have anchored themselves so deeply and dearly in the heart and palate – and world-wide to boot.

It's no wonder that the fried starch suppliers have at-tained the rank of a national treasure in Belgium and are therefore really only comparable to the English Crown, the Brandenburg Gate, and the Statue of Liberty in status. All complete sensory failures though.

Here, it is unfortunately only politically correct and there-fore culinarily correct for children to confess that french fries are their favorite dish – and then only if it can be proven more or less justifiably through membership in a sports club that no risk of imminent obesity is expected. If you have outgrown childhood and come out as a fan of french fries, you won't have to wait long for veritable avalanches of good advice on healthy diets up to possible disease scenarios to be triggered and threaten to always connect eating french fries with a bad conscience. Comfort eating with announcement.

The coolest French fry destroyers

And it is so tasty, this Belgian invention that for its rise into nobility barely escaped the hot frying oil, then is again thoroughly immersed in equally delicious sauces that are not suspected of receiving medals in low-fat rankings.

Here too you can be a bit jealous of the neighbors. Especially when you consider the way the fries look. While they have a tendency to be exiled into the group of substantial proletarian dishes in Germany, you can experience a real treat in Belgium that is hardly conceivable in the upscale gastronomy in this country and is likely to trigger a real affront when attempting to order: Lightly braised pork jowls with a robust red wine sauce and as the side dish – yes, precisely, there they were again, fries. Grandiose. Fantastic. Indescribable. And just the idea that along with just those pork jowls a German restaurant, potentially worthy of stars, would serve potato foam, lets forget any spinal disk problems and follow the potholes to Belgium – towards the most liberal culinary french fry indulgence in the world.

Which finally gets us to the point that the following pages are meant to cover: for those short weekends when a trip to the neighboring country is too long, we have created and refined lots of recipes surrounding potato sticks and when our enthusiasm to experiment occasionally got the better of us we only included those recipes in our little collection that still delighted us in less enthusiastic phases – honestly. And all this without calorie charts and flashing cholesterol-warnings. Simply for feasting.

Marabel

Cheyenne

Gala

Vitelotte

ALL POTATOES
ARE NOT CREATED
EQUAL...

Agria

Worldwide about 300 million tons of potatoes are harvested annually; in Germany alone over 150 varieties are sold. This makes the potato much more than an affordable, filling side dish. It is an important foundation for our daily nourishment. But does the potato really exist? The over 4,000 known varieties worldwide display great variety in appearance, characteristics, and taste despite their similarity. And – starting with a handful of original varieties – geneticists are today still researching more robust, more productive, and more delicate varieties.

Potatoes can be classified according to very different types of characteristics: the color of their skins, the color of their flesh, the shape of their tubers, their starch content, or even the consistency of their skin.

However, generally accepted is a classification by their cooking characteristics. In the EU three types are distinguished that are labeled with the letters A to C:

Firm Potatoes
(Type A and A-B,
color coding: green):
These potatoes, such as the Adelina, Cilena, Hansa, Nicola, Princess, Renate, Selma or Sieglinde varieties have a firm, fine-grained flesh with a moist consistency. Their shape varies from oblong to oval, their flavor is mild to strong. These firm varieties do not blister when cooking and are therefore ideal for salad, fried potatoes or au gratin potatoes.

Predominantly Firm Potatoes
(Type B-A and B,
Color coding: red):
Varieties such as Agria, Bamberger Hörnchen, Berber, Gala, Granola, Laura, Marabel, Quarta, Rita or Solara are characterized by moderately moist and fine-grained flesh with mild to strong flavor. Their shape can vary greatly. During cooking they only blister minimally so they are particularly well suited for boiled potatoes and potatoes in the skin, fried potatoes and soups.

Floury Potatoes
(Type B-C and C,
Color coding: blue):
The similarities of these coarse grained varieties are their dry consistency and their pleasantly strong flavor. The shape of the varieties Adretta, Afra, Bintje, Blue Swede, Karlena, Lakaria, Pirol or Schwarzblaue (blackish-blue) from the Franconian Forest can vary greatly though. The flesh that is light and floury when cooked is particularly suitable for foam or stews.

The cooking properties depend on the starch content and texture. As a general rule: the more starch a potato contains, the more floury it becomes during cooking. Ideal for french fries are potato varieties with a high starch content of about 14–18 percent and low sugar content with a maximum of 0.3 percent. The high starch content ensures a large yield of crispy french fries with good texture and the best flavor. If the sugar content is too high though, the french fries turn brown and bitter during deep-frying.

Freshly harvested varieties are for sale during the months of June to October, stored goods from November to May. Due to their high water content, freshly harvested potatoes are not suitable for deep-frying until after a prolonged storage time. To prevent germination of the tubers, it is best to always store potatoes in a dark and cool place.

VARIETIES SUITABLE FOR DEEP-FRYING

AGRIA

Skin: yellow, rough
Flesh color: yellow
Shape: small tubers, round oval
Cooking type: predominantly firm to floury
Maturity group: medium-early to late

MARABEL

Skin: yellow, smooth
Flesh color: yellow
Shape: medium tubers, round oval
Cooking type: predominantly firm
Maturity group: early

GALA

Skin: yellow, smooth
Flesh color: yellow
Shape: medium to large tubers, round
Cooking type: predominantly firm
Maturity group: early

BINTJE

Skin: yellow, rough
Flesh color: yellow
Shape: medium tubers, round oval
Cooking type: predominantly firm to floury
Maturity group: medium-early is the temperature

However, potatoes are – on the outside as well as the inside – not always yellow. As "Exotic Varieties" we are depicting a red and a blue variety here; they couldn't be any more different:

CHEYENNE

Skin: red, smooth
Flesh color: yellow
Shape: medium tubers, oblong
Cooking type: firm
Maturity group: medium-early

VITELOTTE

noble original potato
Skin: blue, smooth
Flesh color: blue
Shape: small tubers, oblong, deep eyes
Cooking type: firm
Maturity group: late

Sunflower Oil

Olive Oil

Grapeseed oil

Rapeseed
Oil

Avocado Oil

Peanut Oil

... AND FAT IS NOT EQUAL FAT

Nutritional fat and oils have an important role in our nutrition. As important energy suppliers of on average 38.9 kilojoules (9 kcal) per gram they provide fat soluble vitamins, essential fatty acids as well as flavors and aromatic substances. They act as protective and storage substances and improve the texture.

In order to be usable in the kitchen, fats and oils must fulfill a few qualitative criteria. These include stability with respect to heat, aroma and taste, consistent quality and a long shelf life. Even after prolonged use there must not be any formation of smoke and the oil or fat has to avoid oxidative degradation, that is: It must not turn rancid.

Misuse such as heating it to too high or contamination lead to an unpleasant taste or odor, to discolorations, to the formation of smoke, burning or shortened shelf life.

Smoke Points
The temperature, at which an oil or fat starts to smoke, is called a "smoke point." The respective portion of very short-chain fatty acids, e.g. butanoic acid in butter, or free fatty acids in pure fats and oils, lead to lower smoke points. As a rule native oils start smoking at lower temperatures already as raffinates.

Reheating, e.g., when deep-frying, leads to a higher content of free fatty acids. This explains why oils and fats that have been reheated several times already start smoking at lower temperatures.

Refined peanut oil	445°F (230°C)
Refined rape seed oil	430°F (220°C)
Palm kernel oil	430°F (220°C)
Soy oil	415°F (213°C)
Refined sunflower oil	410-440°F (210-225°C)
Ghee	390-400°F (200-205°C)
Refined oils	over 390°F (200°C)
Coconut oil	365-400°F (185-205°C)
Sesame oil	350°F (177°C)
Butter	approx. 350°F (175°C)
Thistle oil	300°F (150°C)
Cold pressed rapeseed oil	265-375°F (130-190°C)
Cold pressed olive oil	265-350°F (130-175°C)
Pork drippings	250-425°F (120-218°C)
Cold pressed sunflower oil	225°F (107°C)

Melting Points
The so-called melting point is respectively the temperature at which the oil or fat transitions from the solid into the liquid state.

Beef tallow	105-120°F (40-50°C)
Palm kernel oil	77-86°F (25-30°C)
Palm oil	86-99°F (30-37°C)
Pork drippings	82-120°F (28-40°C)
Butter	82-100°F (28-38°C)
Coconut oil	64-73°F (18-23°C)
Plant oil	14-34°F (-10-1°C)

WHICH FAT OR OIL FOR WHAT PURPOSE

BUTTER

Contains water, egg white and salt
- ✪ foams and splashes at high temperatures
- ✪ has a low smoke point
- ✪ burns at higher temperatures
- ✪ has a high amount of fatty acid
  Butter therefore is particularly suited for baking or frying at low temperatures.

CLARIFIED BUTTER

Nearly pure fat
- ✪ does not splash
- ✪ has a high smoke point
- ✪ can be heated to a high temperature
- ✪ has a high amount of saturated fatty acids
- ✪ Clarified butter is thus well suited for frying, deep-frying or baking.

LARD/ BEEF TALLOW

Pure fat
- ✪ almost free of water and protein
- ✪ can be heated to a high temperature
- ✪ has a high smoke point
- ✪ has a high amount of saturated fatty acids
- ✪ Lard or beef tallow is thus well suited to pan-frying or deep-frying.

VEGETABLE FAT

Fat with natural solidity: coconut or palm kernel fat Hydrogenated fat: Peanut fat
- ✪ pure fat
- ✪ is not solid
- ✪ does not splash at high temperatures
- ✪ have a high amount of
- ✪ saturated fatty acids
- ✪ can be heated to a high temperature
- ✪ have a high melting point
- ✪ have a high smoke point
- ✪ are tasteless
- ✪ have a long shelf life

Vegetable fat is thus well suited for deep-frying or as a baking or roasting fat.

VEGETABLE OILS

(Palm oil, peanut oil, soybean oil, olive oil, sesame oil, linseed oil, sunflower oil, canola oil)
- ✪ are liquid
- ✪ do not contain water
- ✪ have a high amount of mono- and poly-unsaturated fatty acids

LARD   **OIL**

Cold-pressed vegetable oils are distinguished by their typical, variety-specific taste and smell, and a typical color. The smoke point can be low, however.

Fancy vegetable oils are neutral in taste and smell and colorless. Their smoke point is generally above 390°F (200 °C).

Vegetable oils are therefore only used as a frying oil, if the content of polyunsaturated fatty acids is not too high. Using, e.g. linseed oil or safflower oil is therefore not reasonable. Cold-pressed oils principally work as well for frying as refined oils. Using cold-pressed oils gives the deep-fried food a variety-specific flavor.

From a nutritional perspective, vegetable oils are best suited to deep-frying since they contain fewer saturated and polyunsaturated fatty acids. Particularly recommended are olive oil, canola oil and sunflower oil – however, with olive oil you have to pay close attention to the temperature.

Particularly well suited for deep-frying:
- Vegetable fat
- Vegetable oil
- Refined peanut oil
- Clarified butter

Well suited are:
- Refined canola oil
- Sunflower oil

Suitable are:
- Cold-pressed olive oil
- Cold-pressed canola oil

Not suitable are:
- Butter
- Linseed oil
- Safflower oil

Coconut Oil

Beef Tallow

Vegetable Fat

Pork Drippings

Clarified Butter

GUIDE TO
BEING HAPPY

Deep-frying is primarily a dehydration process: the water contained in the potato and its water soluble ingredients transfer to the fat. The potato absorbs fat, it penetrates into its cavities and cooks from the inside. At the same time, the pores close on the surface and a crust forms so no additional fat can penetrate. So the inside of each individual potato stick reaches about 212°F (100 °C).

For comparison here is the fat content before and after deep-frying:

Potato chips: raw: 0.1 %
French fries: raw: 0.1 %
Deep-fried: 39.8 %
deep-fried: 13.2 %

1. Whatever shape you prefer for your french fries – long and thin or thick, round, wavy or innovative Belgian –you should peel the potatoes first before shaping them.
2. Wash off the starch and let the french fries dry. Please do not place them on paper towels though, since the raw potatoes will then suck up the moisture again.
3. Preheat your deep fryer for several minutes at 140°F (60°C) to heat up the oil or fat.
4. Then heat your deep fryer to 284-350°F (140–180°C.)
5. Fill your deep fryer's frying basket at a maximum to a ratio of fat to food to be fried of 10:1.
6. Possibly shake off coatings, crumbs or other easily removable small parts.
7. Place the deep-frying basket into the hot oil. Carefully shake it so the french fries don't stick to it but float freely in the oil.
8. Deep-fry the french fries for several minutes to cook the inside of the potato sticks.
9. Remove the deep-frying basket from the deep fryer and let the french fries drip dry and cool off for several minutes.
10. Heat your deep fryer to 350-375°F (180–190°C).
11. Deep-fry the french fries for several minutes. They are done when they float on top and have a yellow-gold crust.
12. Remove the frying basket from the deep fryer and sprinkle salt or other spices on the slightly moist french fries.

Why are we telling you at the beginning of a chapter about the fat content of the beloved starch supplier – and on top of that a chapter entitled "Guide to Being Happy"?

After all, more important and interesting are the practical tips regarding deep-frying temperatures and potato architectures. That's why we want to start giving you the first generally applicable instruction for the ultimate crispy french fries at once – precise information can be found in the French Fry Architecture chapter under the respective cutting types.

Double frying at different temperatures prevents the french fries from not being done on the inside or turning too dark on the outside. Please make sure that you do not dip your frying basket into the bubbling fat too full. While the desire to prepare entire mountains of eating pleasure quickly is understandable – the oil simply cools off too fast, which results in it taking longer and leads to a less perfect result because the french fries soak up too much fat since a protective crust cannot form instantly.

You can change the exact deep-frying temperatures depending on the type of potato and oil used and the location of the deep fryer (inside or outside) and the associated weather conditions. The temperatures listed therefore are geared towards the average.

French fries from the freezer as a rule are frozen after the first deep-frying pass and thus only have to be deep-fried once. Definitely thaw frozen french fries beforehand and let them dry briefly. Otherwise they will cool down the oil too much and the large amount of moisture will have the fat dangerously close to bubbling and steaming.

Before warming up your deep fryer check the oil. If it smells or tastes unpleasant, it must be replaced. If there is smoke or foam development during heating, it should be replaced. Also check the fill level and add

any missing amount. Dark coloring on the other hand is not necessarily an indication of poor quality. It can be the result of a reaction of protein substances with fat components or sugar, which is harmless for further use.

However, dark coloration due to food remnants is different. They continue to be fried in the hot oil and thus cause bitter aromas long-term. The oil should therefore be freed from remnants with a heat resistant filter after each deep-frying pass.

Vegetables, fish, meat, etc., should always be deep-fried separately. Please dry off wet food beforehand. Frozen products should be thawed and dried before deep-frying. Crumbs, coatings and other easily removed small parts should be shaken off before deep-frying. Deep-fried dishes should always be salted or spiced only after deep-frying.

Please let the deep-fried food dry sufficiently after deep-frying. Cover the deep fryer to protect it from contamination. If you take longer breaks during cooking, lower the temperature of the deep fryer to about 140°F (60°C). During shorter breaks, close the deep fryer and maintain the temperature. However, the most important tip for uniform quality of the french fries is: clean your deep fryer thoroughly and always replace the oil or fat in time!

And now: Enjoy!

CLASSIC

To enjoy real Belgian french fries you do not have to embark on a special trip to Belgium. With this simple recipe they can be easily prepared at home. Originally, deep-frying in beef suet gave Belgian potato sticks their incomparable taste. Today, though, vegetable fat tends to be used. However, the fat is not the only key to real Belgian ones, the proper type of potato and, of course, preparation is important too!

INGREDIENTS FOR 2 SERVINGS

1 lb. (500 g) potatoes, floury (e.g. Bintje)
salt, coarse-grained

PREPARATION

○ Peel and wash the potatoes and cut them into finger-thick slices, then again into sticks.
○ Wash the potato sticks thoroughly to rinse out the potato starch. Then dry them well while wrapped in a kitchen towel so there won't be any splashing while deep-frying.
○ Heat the prepared deep fryer to approx. 280-300°F (140–150°C).
○ Place half of the french fries into the frying basket and lower it into the hot oil. Carefully shake the basket while doing this so the french fries don't stick to the basket but swim freely in the fat.
○ Deep-fry the french fries for approx. 6 minutes.
○ Remove the frying basket from the oil, let the french fries drip dry and then place them on a paper towel for further drying.
○ Repeat the process with the second half of the prepared french fries.

○ Increase the temperature of the deep-frying fat to 350-375°F (175–190°C).
○ Place the first half of the prefried french fries into the frying basket and deep-fry them for about 1 minute until they are floating on top and take on a golden yellow color. Then place them into a sieve for draining.
○ Repeat the process with the second half of the prefried french fries. Make sure the deep-frying fat reheats to the desired temperature between deep-frying passes.
○ Salt the Belgian french fries lightly and serve them still hot – for example with a fruity-piquant fig sauce. *(See recipe page 54)*

SLIM

The typical long thin ones are nice and crispy on the outside and wonderfully potatoey on the inside. The trick is deep-frying them twice! For in a single deep-frying pass they would either not be done on the inside or be too dark on the outside.

INGREDIENTS FOR 2 SERVINGS

1 lb. (500 g) large potatoes, predominantly firm (e.g. Gala)

salt or spice powder at will

PREPARATION

- Peel and wash the potatoes and cut them into approx. ¹/₃ inch (1 cm)-thick slices to begin with, then again into approx. ¹/₃ inch (1 cm)-wide sticks.
- Wash the potato sticks thoroughly to rinse off the potato starch. Then dry them well while wrapped in a kitchen towel so there won't be any splashing while deep-frying.
- Heat the prepared deep fryer to approx. 280-300°F (140–150°C).
- Place half of the french fries into the frying basket and lower it into the hot oil. Carefully shake the basket so the french fries don't stick to the basket but swim freely in the fat.
- Deep-fry for approx. 4 minutes.
- Remove the frying basket from the oil, let the french fries drip dry and then place them on a paper towel for further drying.
- Repeat the process with the second half of the prepared french fries.

- Increase the temperature of the deep-frying fat to 350-375°F (175–190°C).
- Place the first half of the prefried french fries into the frying basket and deep-fry them for about 1 minute until they are floating on top and take on a golden yellow color. Then place them into a sieve for draining.
- Repeat the process with the second half of the prefried french fries. Make sure the deep-frying fat reheats to the desired temperature between deep-frying passes.
- Spice the long thin ones with salt and paprika powder and serve them hot – for example with a fruity spicy habanero foam. *(See recipe page 54)*

ROUND

In this round, crispy delight the potato shows itself from one of its best sides: on the inside almost creamy like a puree but on the outside crispy!

INGREDIENTS FOR 2 SERVINGS
2.2 lbs. (1 kg) potatoes, floury (e.g. Bintje)
salt

PREPARATION

- Peel and wash the potatoes. Then cut smalls balls out of the potato flesh with a round melon baller. Press the melon baller deep into the potato flesh and loosen the ball with a twist.
- Let the potato balls fall into cold water and thoroughly rinse off the potato starch. Then dry the balls well while wrapped in a kitchen towel so there won't be any splashing while deep-frying.
- Heat the prepared deep fryer to approx. 280-300°F (140–150°C).
- Place half of the french fry balls into the frying basket and lower it into the hot oil. Carefully shake the basket so the balls don't stick to the basket but swim freely in the fat.
- Deep-fry the balls for approx. 6 minutes.
- Remove the frying basket from the oil, let the balls drip dry, and then place them on a paper towel for further drying.
- Repeat the process with the second half of the prepared potato balls.
- Increase the temperature of the deep-frying fat to 350-375°F (175–190°C).
- Place the first half of the prefried balls into the frying basket and deep-fry them for about 2 minutes until they are floating on top and take on a golden yellow color. Then place them into a sieve for draining.
- Repeat the process with the second half of the prefried french fry balls. Make sure the deep-frying fat reheats to the desired temperature between deep-frying passes.
- Spice the balls with salt and paprika powder and serve them hot – for example with a tasty paprika dip. *(See recipe page 48)*

> **TIP:** Save the remaining potato shells covered with cold water and use them for potato soup or puree the next day.

The potato balls can also be prepared in a little oil or butter in a pan. Place as many balls in the hot oil as can fit in one layer next to each other. Turn the balls by quickly pulling on the panhandle, but keep a close eye on them: The French Fries Parisienne are done faster than one might think!

PUFFED UP

In this type of unusual preparation the potato slices puff up to airy, light potato pillows. Classically they accompany a juicy Chateaubriand, but they are also very well suited as a main dish on their own or as an accompaniment to dips and sauces.

INGREDIENTS FOR 2 SERVINGS

1 lb. (500 g) potatoes, floury

PREPARATION

○ Peel and wash the potatoes and cut them into approx. 1 inch (3 cm)-thick slices.

○ Wash the potato slices thoroughly to rinse off the starch. Then dry them well while wrapped in a kitchen towel so there won't be any splashing while deep-frying.

○ Heat the prepared deep fryer to approx. 350°F (175°C).

○ Place half of the french fries into the frying basket and lower into the hot oil. Carefully shake the basket while doing this so the french fries don't stick to the basket but swim freely in the fat.

○ Deep-fry for about 3 minutes.

○ Remove the frying basket from the oil, let the french fries drip dry, and then place them on a paper towel for further drying.

○ Repeat the process with the second half of prepared french fries.

○ Increase the temperature of the deep-frying fat to 355-375°F (180–190°C).

○ Place the first half of the prefried french fries into the frying basket and deep-fry them for about 1 minute until they are floating on top and take on a golden yellow color. Then place them into a sieve for draining.

○ Repeat the process with the second half of the prefried french fries. Make sure the deep-frying fat reheats to the desired temperature between deep-frying passes.

○ Lightly salt the french fry soufflés and serve them hot – for example with a cold pea sauce.

DYNAMICALLY
WRAPPED

This french fry variation is reminiscent of long evenings at the campfire, grilled sausages on sticks or campfire twist bread. Potatoes don't want to always just lie in the embers boringly wrapped in aluminum foil either ...

INGREDIENTS FOR 2 SERVINGS

2 large potatoes, floury to predominantly firm

PREPARATION

- ✪ Peel and wash the potatoes and cut them into one endless spiral each using a radish slicer.
- ✪ Carefully place the spirals onto suitable sticks or even several wooden skewers.
- ✪ Heat the prepared deep fryer to approx. 285-300°F (140–150°C).
- ✪ Place the potato spirals into the frying basket individually and lower it into the hot oil. Carefully shake the basket while doing this so they don't stick to the basket but swim freely in the fat.
- ✪ Deep-fry the tornado for approx. 6 minutes.
- ✪ Remove the frying basket from the oil, let the skewer drip dry, and then place it on a paper towel for further drying.

- ✪ Repeat the process with the second skewer.
- ✪ Increase the temperature of the deep-frying fat to 350-375°F (175–190°C).
- ✪ Place the first tornado into the frying basket and deep-fry it for about 1 minute until it floats on top and takes on a golden yellow color. Then place it into a sieve for draining.
- ✪ Repeat the process with the second skewer. Make sure the deep-frying fat reheats to the desired temperature between deep-frying passes.
- ✪ Lightly salt the tornado and serve hot – for example with a tomato based hot sauce. *(See recipe page 47)*

PARMESAN !

ENDLESS

This variation on spaghetti doesn't just make kids' hearts beat faster! Admittedly, they can't be twirled onto a fork as nicely but they are much crispier ...

INGREDIENTS FOR 2 SERVINGS
2 large potatoes, floury to predominantly firm

PREPARATION

- Peel and wash the potatoes. Cut the potatoes using a spaghetti spiral cutter into one endless spiral each.
- Rinse the "spaghetti" under running water and place them in nests onto paper towels or kitchen towels for drying.
- Heat the prepared deep fryer to approx. 285-300°F (140–150°C).
- Place the potato nests into the frying basket individually and lower it into the hot oil. Carefully shake the basket while doing this so they don't stick to the basket but swim freely in the fat.
- Deep-fry the spaghetti nests for approx. 3 minutes.
- Remove the frying basket from the oil, let the nests drip dry and then place them on a paper towel for further drying.
- Repeat the process with the second potato nest.
- Increase the temperature of the deep-frying fat to 350-375°F (175–190°C).
- Place the first nest into the frying basket and deep-fry it for about 1 minute until it floats on top and takes on a golden yellow color. Then place it into a sieve for draining.
- Repeat the process with the second potato nest. Make sure the deep-frying fat reheats to the desired temperature between deep-frying passes.
- Lightly salt the "spaghetti" and serve it hot – for example completely traditional with ketchup and a bit of freshly ground parmesan.

ENERGETICALLY CURLED

INGREDIENTS FOR 2 SERVINGS

10 small potatoes, floury

PREPARATION

- ✪ Peel and wash the potatoes. Cut them into tight spirals using a potato spiral.
- ✪ Wash the potato curls thoroughly to rinse off the potato starch. Then dry them well while wrapped in a kitchen towel so there won't be any splashing while deep-frying.
- ✪ Heat the prepared deep fryer to approx. 285-300°F (140–150°C).
- ✪ Place half of the french fry curls into the frying basket and lower it into the hot oil. Carefully shake the basket while doing this so they don't stick to the basket but swim freely in the fat.
- ✪ Deep-fry the french fries for approx. 6 minutes.
- ✪ Remove the frying basket from the oil, let the french fry spirals drip dry and then place them on a paper towel for further drying.
- ✪ Repeat the process with the second half of the prepared curls.

- ✪ Increase the temperature of the deep-frying fat to 350-375°F (175–190°C).
- ✪ Place the first half of the prefried french fries into the frying basket and deep-fry them for about 1 minute until they are floating on top and take on a golden yellow color. Then place them into a sieve for draining.
- ✪ Repeat the process with the second half of the prefried French fry spirals. Make sure the deep-frying fat reheats to the desired temperature between deep-frying passes.
- ✪ Salt the energetically curled french fries lightly and serve them hot – for example with a wonderful curry-pineapple dip. *(See recipe page 53)*

INNOVATIVE

A dream for all sauce junkies: french fries for dipping! Due to their V-shaped preparation they serve as spoons at the same time and make scooping up sauces, dips, and small accompaniments marvelously easy.

INGREDIENTS FOR 2 SERVINGS

1 lb. (500 g) potatoes, predominantly firm

PREPARATION

- Peel and wash the potatoes and cut them into finger-thick slices, then into sticks using a V-shaped carving knife.
- Wash the potato sticks thoroughly to rinse off the starch. Then dry them well while wrapped in a kitchen towel so there won't be any splashing while deep-frying.
- Heat the prepared deep fryer to approx. 285-300°F (140–150°C).
- Place half of the french fries into the frying basket and lower it into the hot oil. Carefully shake the basket while doing this so the french fries don't stick to the basket but swim freely in the fat.
- Deep-fry the french fries for approx. 4 minutes.
- Remove the frying basket from the oil, let the french fries drip dry and then place them on a paper towel for further drying.

- Repeat the process with the second half of the prepared french fries.
- Increase the temperature of the deep-frying fat to 350-375°F (175–190°C).
- Place the first half of the prefried french fries into the frying basket and deep-fry them for about 1 minute until they are floating on top and take on a golden yellow color. Then place them into a sieve for draining.
- Repeat the process with the second half of the prefried french fries. Make sure the deep-frying fat reheats to the desired temperature between deep-frying passes.
- Lightly salt these unusual french fries and serve them hot – for example with a nutty, spicy peanut sauce, a cajun sauce or a pinapple dip. *(See recipe pages 52 and 53)*

SAUCES

KETCHUP FOR ALL

INGREDIENTS

1 1/3 lb. (600 g) ripe tomatoes

1/3 lb. (150 g) red onions,
  coarsely chopped

2 cloves of garlic, coarsely chopped

1 small red chili pepper,
  alternatively one dried

2 star anis

5 pimento corns

some ginger powder

1/2 cinnamon stick

3 1/3 ounces (100 ml) red wine vinegar

1/4 cup (50 g) raw cane sugar

11/2–2 tbsp starch

PREPARATION

❂ Remove the stem starts from the
  tomatoes, score the skin all the way
  around several times, pour boiling
  water over them and peel. Quarter,
  remove the seeds and then puree
  together with the garlic and onions.
  Put the pureed tomatoes in a pot,
  add the spices, mix thoroughly with
  the tomato onion mixture and let it
  simmer for 30–40 minutes while stirring frequently.

❂ Then put the tomatoes through a
  coarse sieve and bring to a boil in
  a different pot together with the
  sugar and vinegar and let it simmer
  another 10 minutes while stirring
  repeatedly. Now blend the starch
  with cold water and add to the cooking tomatoes.

❂ Bring everything to a boil again and
  then immediately fill into sterilized
  jars or bottles.

MAYONNAISE

INGREDIENTS

2 egg yolk

1 cup (about 250 ml) cold-pressed
  vegetable oil, e.g. canola oil

2 tbsp Dijon mustard

dash lemon juice

dash Worcestershire sauce

1 pinch of cayenne pepper

1 pinch of sugar

salt

pepper

PREPARATION

❂ Remove the eggs from the refrigerator in time to reach room temperature before processing. Mix the egg
  yolk and mustard together and beat
  with the mixer. Slowly let the oil
  flow into the mixture and continue
  mixing until the desired consistency
  has been obtained. At the end stir
  in lemon juice, salt, pepper and
  cayenne pepper, sugar and Worcestershire sauce.

PINK BERRY

INGREDIENTS FOR 4 SERVINGS

6 tbsp mayonnaise *(see recipe page 38)*

2 tbsp Dijon mustard

1 clove of garlic, crushed

2 sprigs Italian parsley, finely chopped

2 tsp lemon juice

2 tbsp Worcestershire sauce

2 tsp pink berries or red pepper,
  ground in a mortar

PREPARATION

✪ Thoroughly mix all ingredients together and let them meld a bit before
  serving.

HONEY MUSTARD DIP WITH ONIONS

INGREDIENTS FOR 4 SERVINGS

6 tbsp medium sharp mustard

2 tbsp honey (preferrably liquid
  honey, if only solid is available,
  mix it with some hot water)

1 tsp voatsiperifery pepper,
  ground in the mortar

2 tbsp mayonnaise *(see recipe page 38)*

2 onions, cut in half and
  then cut into semicircles

2–3 tbsp canola oil

2 tbsp sugar

PREPARATION

✪ Heat the canola oil in the pan and
  slowly sautée the onion rings. Add
  the sugar and let all of it turn golden
  yellow and crispy. Chill.
✪ Mix all other ingredients together
  and stir the onions into the sauce
  right before serving.

Bell Pepper Buttermilk

Honey Mustard

Gold Pea

Pink Berry

40

BELL PEPPER BUTTERMILK DIP

INGREDIENTS FOR 4 SERVINGS

3 sweet red bell peppers,
    cut in half and deseeded
1 tsp sharp mustard
1 tsp mustard seed, ground in mortar
1 tbsp white balsamic vinegar
1/2 tbsp chives
1/2 tbsp Italian parsley, finely chopped
1/2 clove of garlic, crushed
1/2 red chili pepper, very finely chopped
1/3 cup (80 ml) buttermilk
2 tbsp mayonnaise *(see recipe page 38)*
a bit of canola oil

PREPARATION

✪ Heat a bit of canola oil in the pan
and sear the bell pepper halves until
the skin starts to separate. After
they cool down, peel off the skin and
puree with an immersion blender.
Add all other ingredients and mix
thoroughly.

COLD PEA

INGREDIENTS FOR 4 SERVINGS

1 cup (150 g) peas, frozen, thawed
4 sprigs mint, finely chopped
2 sprigs coriander, finely chopped
1/2 habanero, deseeded
    and very finely chopped
3 tbsp whipped cream
1 tsp horseradish or wasabi paste
1 tbsp white balsamic vinegar
2 tbsp mayonnaise *(see recipe page 38)*

PREPARATION

✪ Mix all ingredients together except
for the mayonnaise, puree and season with salt to taste. Then stir in the
mayonnaise and chill until served.

BÉARNAISE SAUCE

INGREDIENTS FOR 4 SERVINGS

1 cup (220 g) butter
⅓ cup (70 ml) dry white wine
¼ (40 ml) cup water
2 shallots, finely chopped
½ tsp crushed black peppercorns
½ bunch tarragon, destemmed
3 egg yolks
salt
lemon juice
pinch of cayenne pepper

PREPARATION

- Melt 14 tablespoons of the butter in a pot. In a second pot, brown the shallots in the remaining butter, deglaze with the white wine and water and bring to a boil briefly. Add the pepper and let it cool off a bit. Then whip with the egg yolk in the water-bath into a homogeneous mass without bringing it to a boil. Remove from the stove and while stirring continuously let the molten butter flow very slowly into the egg mixture.
- Finely chop the tarragon and stir it into the finished sauce and season everything to taste with salt, cayenne pepper and some lemon juice.

CURRY MAYONNAISE

INGREDIENTS FOR 4 SERVINGS

2 egg yolk
7 ounces (200 ml) sunflower oil
1 tbsp sharp mustard
1 squirt white wine vinegar
1 tsp curry
salt
pepper

PREPARATION

- Take the eggs out of the refrigerator in time to reach room temperature. Thoroughly mix the egg yolk with the mustard, then add the vinegar, salt and pepper. Add the oil very slowly and mix it with the mixer until the desired consistency has been reached. Then add the curry powder and mix again. Season to taste with salt and pepper.

AIOLI DE LUXE

INGREDIENTS FOR 4 SERVINGS

2 large egg yolk
1 cup (250 ml) olive oil
½ tsp sugar
1 tbsp lemon juice
1 clove of garlic, very finely chopped
2 pinches of curry powder
1 pinch saffron
pepper

PREPARATION

✪ Take the eggs out of the refrigerator in time to reach room temperature. Mix the chopped garlic with the egg yolk, sugar and a pinch of salt. Then let the olive oil drip slowly into the mixture and mix it with a mixer. Then mix in the lemon juice, curry powder and saffron and finally season to taste with salt and pepper.

GINGER MAYONNAISE

INGREDIENTS FOR 4 SERVINGS

½ cup (120 g) mayonnaise
  (see recipe Page 38)
1 shallot, peeled and quartered
1 red chili pepper, cut in
  half lengthwise and deseeded
approx. ⅓ inch (1 cm) ginger,
  peeled, coarsely chopped
1 tbsp lime juice
1 tbsp sesame oil
1 tsp fish sauce
1 tsp light-colored soybean sauce

PREPARATION

✪ Place all ingredients together in a mixer and mix. Let them meld a bit before serving.

Cashew Olive Dip

Tartar Sauce

Rosemary Mayonn

TARTAR SAUCE

INGREDIENTS FOR 4 SERVINGS

1 ⅛ cup (250 g) sour cream

5 tbsp mayonnaise *(see recipe page 38)*

1 tsp capers, chopped

1 shallot, finely chopped

1 tbsp lemon juice

2 pickled cucumbers, finely diced

2 tbsp chives

1 tsp Dijon mustard

salt

pepper

cayenne pepper

PREPARATION

✪ Mix the sour cream with the mayonnaise, add all other ingredients and mix thoroughly. Season to taste with salt, pepper and cayenne pepper and let it meld. Possibly add more seasoning before serving.

ROSEMARY MAYONNAISE

INGREDIENTS FOR 4 SERVINGS

1 large egg yolk

3 ⅓ ounces (100 ml)
  canola oil, cold-pressed

1 tsp mustard

a touch of lemon juice

2–3 sprigs rosemary

salt

pepper

PREPARATION

✪ Heat the oil in a pot while making
sure that it is not too hot. Place the
rosemary sprigs in warm oil, cover
the pot with the lid and let the rosemary soak for two to three hours in
the oil. Remove the sprigs. Then mix
the egg yolk with the mustard, drip
in the oil a drop at a time and continue to stir with the mixer until the
desired consistency is reached. Then
mix in the lemon juice and season to
taste with salt and pepper.

CASHEW OLIVE DIP

INGREDIENTS FOR 4 SERVINGS

2 tbsp cashew kernels (gladly
  cashew pieces too), coarsely chopped

approx. 10–12 green olives,
  coarsely chopped

4–5 tbsp Italian parsley, chopped

3 tbsp sunflower oil

3 tbsp mayonnaise *(see recipe page 38)*

3 squirt Worcestershire sauce

PREPARATION

✪ Puree the nuts together with the
olives and the parsley while adding
the oil. Add the Worcestershire sauce
and mix. Then stir in the mayonnaise and let it meld a little before
serving.

TOMATO BASED

Barbecue Sauce

Spicy Tomato Sauce

BARBECUE SAUCE

INGREDIENTS FOR 4 SERVINGS

6 ¾ ounces (200 ml) ketchup *(see recipe page 38)*

2 oranges, preferably juice oranges

1–2 slices pineapple

3 tbsp Worcestershire sauce

1 red chili pepper, small, deseeded
   and finely chopped

1 red onion, diced

3 tbsp maple syrup

a bit of oil

salt

pepper

PREPARATION

✪ Squeeze the oranges and set aside ⅓ cup (100 ml) juice. Dice the pineapple, then heat the oil in the pan and steam the onions in it. Add the pineapple, maple syrup, ketchup, the chili pepper and the Worcestershire sauce to the onions in the pan and let it simmer a few minutes at medium temperature. Strain the sauce through a sieve that isn't too fine, let it cool and season to taste with salt and pepper before serving.

ZESTY KETCHUP

INGREDIENTS FOR 4 SERVINGS

1 lb. (500 g) ripe tomatoes

4 tbsp sugar

1 tbsp sharp curry powder

1/4 tsp cayenne

1/4 tsp sharp paprika powder

$^1/_2$ red chili pepper, deseeded
and finely chopped

2 tbsp olive oil

2 tbsp white wine vinegar

2 tbsp tomato paste

salt

pepper

PREPARATION

○ Slit the tomatoes crosswise and pour
boiling water over them, deseed and
chop into small pieces. Heat the olive
oil in a pot and heat the tomatoes in
it. Add the sugar, caramelize lightly.
Add the spices and stir in. Then add
the vinegar, tomato paste and chili
pepper, bring to a boil and then
puree it all. Season to taste with salt
and pepper.

SPICY TOMATO SAUCE

INGREDIENTS FOR 4 SERVINGS

2 medium onions, diced

1 small clove of garlic, finely chopped

1 tbsp olive oil

4 tbsp tomato paste

$^1/_3$ pound (150 g) sieved tomatoes

2 tbsp lemon juice

2–3 tbsp soy sauce

1–2 tbsp liquid honey

$^1/_2$ tsp harissa

salt

PREPARATION

○ Steam the onions with the garlic in
the olive oil and then add the tomato
paste and the sieved tomatoes. Let it
simmer for 10 minutes at low heat.
Then add the soy sauce, honey and
harissa paste, stir thoroughly and
season to taste with lemon juice and
salt.

BELL PEPPER DIP

INGREDIENTS FOR 4 SERVINGS

2 red bell peppers
2 tbsp tomato paste
2 tsp soy sauce
2 tsp white balsamic vinegar
paprika, sweet
chili flakes
salt
pepper

PREPARATION

○ Cut the bell pepper in half, deseed, place with the cut edge down on a cookie sheet lined with parchment paper and heat in an oven at approx. 355 °F (180 °C) until the skin loosens.

○ Wrap the bell pepper half in plastic wrap and let it rest for 10 minutes. Then remove the skin and dice the bell pepper into small pieces and mix in a bowl with tomato paste, soy sauce and vinegar. Puree it all and season to taste with salt, pepper and paprika. Make it "hotter" to taste with chili flakes.

ZESTY PAPRIKA ONION DIP

INGREDIENTS FOR 4 SERVINGS

2 onions, very finely diced
1 red bell pepper
1 tsp paprika powder, sweet
$^{1}/_{2}$ tsp harissa
$^{1}/_{2}$ tsp cayenne pepper
1–2 tsp tomato paste
a bit of olive oil

PREPARATION

○ Cut the bell pepper in half, deseed and place with the cut edge down on a parchment paper in the oven that has been preheated to 390 °F (200 °C). As soon as the skin turns dark, take it out, wrap it in plastic wrap and let it rest. Then remove the skin and dice the bell pepper into very small pieces. Add to the diced onions and thoroughly mix with all other ingredients. Those who like it spicy, can add some additional harissa paste.

Bell Pepper Dip

CURRY ORANGE KETCHUP

Zesty Paprika Onion Dip

Ingredients for 4 servings

1 red onion, finely chopped

1 small clove of garlic, finely chopped

6 ³/₄ ounces (200 ml) ketchup *(see recipe Page 38)*

¹/₄ cup (60 ml) orange juice

¹/₂ red chili pepper, deseeded and finely chopped

3 tsp mild curry powder

a bit of olive oil

salt

pepper

Curry Orange Ketchup

PREPARATION

○ Heat the oil in a pan and braise the garlic with the onion until the onion is translucent. Add the orange juice and the ketchup, stir everything, sprinkle the curry powder on top, stir again and bring to a boil briefly. Spice with salt and pepper to taste.

TRENDY

Chocolate Reversed

Chickpea Dip

Peanut Coriander Dip

CHOCOLATE REVERSED

INGREDIENTS FOR 4 SERVINGS

6 tbsp canola oil

1 tsp fennel seed, ground in mortar

$1/2$ cinnamon stick, ground in mortar
  (best is a thin Ceylon cinnamon stick)

1 tsp coriander seeds, ground in mortar

6 $3/4$ ounces (200 ml) Greek yogurt

salt

PREPARATION

✪ Heat the oil in the pan, add the spices, brown lightly and when cooled, stir it into the yoghurt. Season to taste with salt.

CHICKPEA DIP

INGREDIENTS FOR 4 SERVINGS

1 cup (200 g) canned chickpeas

1 clove of garlic, finely chopped

1 tbsp (50 g) sesame paste

2 tbsp lemon juice

2 tbsp olive oil

a bit of cumin

a bit of turmeric

1 tbsp coriander, finely chopped

salt

PREPARATION

✪ Let the chickpeas drain, catch the liquid and set aside. Now puree the chickpeas and stir the garlic, sesame paste, olive oil and lemon juice into the mixture. Stir enough of the drained liquid into the sauce to obtain the desired consistency. Stir in the coriander and season to taste with cumin, turmeric and salt.

PEANUT CORIANDER DIP

INGREDIENTS FOR 4 SERVINGS

$1/2$ lemon, juice

4 tbsp peanuts, unsalted

1 tbsp rice vinegar

1 tbsp Worcestershire sauce

1 tsp honey, liquid

4 tbsp canola oil

2 sprigs coriander

1 tbsp whipped cream

PREPARATION

✪ Finely puree the lemon juice together with the peanuts, the rice vinegar, the Worcestershire sauce, the sesame oil, the honey and 2–3 tbsp water in the mixer. Slowly add the canola oil and continue blending. Then pull the leaves off the coriander sprigs, finely chop them, fold under the mixture and stir in the whipped cream.

Spicy Peanut

Zoe's Cajun Sauce

Curry Pineapple Dip

SPICY PEANUT

INGREDIENTS FOR 4 SERVINGS

6 tbsp peanut butter, crunchy

2 tbsp soy sauce

2 tbsp oyster sauce

2 tsp green curry paste

2 whole allspice seeds,
  ground in mortar

1 clove of garlic, crushed

4 tbsp whipped cream

PREPARATION

✪ Thoroughly mix all ingredients together and add 2 tbsp boiling water.
  Let it meld a bit and then serve.

ZOE'S CAJUN SAUCE

INGREDIENTS FOR 4 SERVINGS

1 stick celery, very finely chopped

1/2 onion, very finely chopped

3 sprigs Italian parsley,
   very finely chopped

1 clove of garlic, crushed

4 tbsp mayonnaise *(see recipe page 38)*

1/2 tsp paprika powder, sweet

1 tsp horseradish

1 tsp Dijon mustard

1 tsp ketchup *(see recipe page 38)*

1 tsp lemon juice

1 tsp Worcestershire sauce

1 tbsp chili sauce, spicy

PREPARATION

✪ Mix all ingredients together and
let the sauce meld before serving.
Those who like it spicier can simply
sprinkle some finely chopped chili
pepper on top.

CURRY PINEAPPLE DIP

INGREDIENTS FOR 4 SERVINGS

4 slices pineapple, canned,
   cut into small pieces

some pineapple juice from the can

1 1/2 tbsp fresh ginger,
   cut into rough slices

1 1/2 tbsp cane sugar

1/2 tsp curry

1 1/2 tbsp crème fraîche

salt

PREPARATION

✪ Crush the pineapple together with
the ginger with a fork and then let it
simmer in a pot with some pineapple juice and the sugar until the
sugar starts caramelizing. Let it cool
and then mix it with all other ingredients. Season to taste with salt. Let
it meld a bit before serving. Those
who like it spicier can sprinkle a bit
of finely chopped red chili pepper
(without seeds) on top.

HABANERO FOAM

INGREDIENTS FOR 4 SERVINGS

2 tsp (10 ml) mild olive oil

2 egg white, almost beaten stiff

2 tsp lemon juice

1 clove of garlic, crushed

½ habanero, very finely chopped

2 tbsp pear juice concentrate or similar

2 tbsp maple syrup

2 tbsp mayonnaise *(see recipe page 38)*

2 tbsp oyster sauce

salt

PREPARATION

✪ Using a whisk slowly stir the oil into the whipped egg white. Then stir in the other ingredients and season to taste with salt.

FIG DIP

INGREDIENTS FOR 4 SERVINGS

4 fresh figs, sliced

1 ½ tbsp butter

1 ½ tsp sugar

1 ½ tsp mustard seed

1 ½ tbsp Worcestershire sauce

salt

PREPARATION

✪ Let the fig melt with the butter and some water in the pot and add the sugar. Watch the mixture: When the sugar starts to caramelize at the edge, take the pot off the stove top. Stir the mustard seed into the still warm mixture and let it cool off. Season to taste with Worcestershire sauce and salt.

FRUITY PEANUT SAUCE

INGREDIENTS FOR 4 SERVINGS

1 cup (250 g) peanut butter

6 ¾ ounces (200 ml) coconut milk

2 cups (500 ml) pineapple juice

1 clove of garlic, very finely chopped

1 tsp curry or harissa paste

2 tsp mango chutney

a bit of starch

PREPARATION

✪ Heat the pineapple juice but do not bring it to a boil. Pour the coconut milk into the hot juice, stir, then dissolve the peanut butter in the mixture. Then mix in the mango chutney, garlic and the spice paste. Dissolve the starch in cold water and thicken the mixture with it until the desired consistency is obtained. Season to taste with additional spice paste depending on how spicy you want it to be.

SWEET POTATO ROYALE

INGREDIENTS FOR 4 SERVINGS

1 cup (200 g) sour cream

1 spring onion, cut into thin rings

8 sprigs Italian parsley, finely chopped

2 tsp lemon juice

1 clove of garlic, crushed

2 tbsp mayonnaise *(see recipe page 38)*

2 pinches sugar

$^1/_2$ tsp turmeric

$^1/_2$ tsp ground allspice

$^1/_2$ tsp cumin

$^1/_2$ tsp coriander seeds,
  ground in mortar

salt

PREPARATION

✪ Thoroughly mix all ingredients
together and salt to taste. Let them
meld a bit before serving.

POUTINE SAUCE

Ingredients for this Quebec national dish can be difficult to find, but a french fry book without this calorie mother ship would definitely raise doubts as to its legitimacy – and what french fry book wants to go down that difficult path? What follows is a rather unusual recipe that in the strictest sense of the word really isn't one but only a description of what makes a poutine and how you can best improvise it.

The essential part of the recipe is gravy, a brown (roast) sauce that you can either mix using instant powder or basically "imitate" by thickening a very strong broth with starch that was stirred into cold water beforehand.

As topping you need cheese curds, so grated cheese in a consistency somewhere between quark and cheddar. A characteristic of this cheese that should not be neglected is that it squeaks when you chew it.

Once you have purchased sauce and cheese in addition to the obligatory french fries (it's best to not get them too thin), everything is very easy: First, layer the sauce on the french fries and cover the whole thing with cheese that then hopefully will give off the appropriate sounds during feasting . . .

INGREDIENTS FOR ABOUT 4 SERVINGS

3 tbsp. peeled hemp nuts (available in health food stores)

1 tbsp. sea salt

½ tbsp. curry

PREPARATION

Roast the hemp nuts without fat in the pan. Then pestle thoroughly together with the salt in a mortar, add the curry powder and mix in evenly.

Sea salt with black sesame

INGREDIENTS FOR ABOUT 4 SERVINGS

3 tbsp. unpeeled sesame

1 tbsp. sea salt

1 tbsp. pink berries

PREPARATION

Roast the sesame without fat in the pan. Then pestle thoroughly together with the salt and the pink berries in a mortar.

Sea salt with sesame and pink berries

INGREDIENTS FOR ABOUT 4 SERVINGS

3 tbsp. black sesame seeds

1 tbsp. sea salt

PREPARATION

Roast the sesame without fat in the pan. Then pestle thoroughly together with the salt in a mortar.

SALTS

French fry salt for the pantry

INGREDIENTS

5 tbsp. sea salt

1 tbsp. smoked salt

2 tbsp. paprika, sweet

½ tbsp. black pepper

½ tbsp. ginger powder

1 tbsp. garlic granules

PREPARATION

Mix all ingredients together thoroughly.

INGREDIENTS

¼ cup (50 g) sea salt

1 twig rosemary, picked off

PREPARATION

Chop the rosemary needles coarsely and pestle them in a mortar. Slowly add the salt and also pestle. Preheat the oven to 85-105 °F (35-40 °C), spread the salt on a baking tray and dry in the oven for about an hour. Stir occasionally with a cooking spoon. Then pour it through a semi-fine sieve. This sieves out the larger rosemary needles.

Rosemary salt for the pantry

SCALLOPED FRENCH FRIES

INGREDIENTS FOR 2 SERVINGS

1 pound (500 g) french fries

1 medium onion

1 clove of garlic

1 slice pork belly or bacon, lightly smoked

2 medium tomatoes

¹/₂ pound (250 g) cheese (e.g. emmentaler, gouda)

a bit of salt and black pepper from the grinder

possibly chili

possibly champignons

PREPARATION

✪ Brown the pork belly that has been cut into small cubes in a coated pan. Add the thin slices of onion and the finely chopped garlic and braise until translucent. Clean the champignons with a small brush if needed, cut them into thin slices and braise them as well. If the pork belly reduces too much fat, drain a portion.

✪ Score the tomatoes, briefly blanch them in cold water and peel. Let the tomatoes cool off briefly, then cut them into small cubes and remove the seeds. Next add them to the pan as well and heat over a medium flame. Pepper the whole thing and only salt lightly. Let the mixture meld and cool off.

✪ Cut the french fries into the desired shape, wash, dry and bake on a baking tray for approx. 15 minutes at 390°F (200°C) until golden yellow, turn once. Spread the prepared bacon mixture over the french fries, grate the cheese on top and continue baking at 355-390°F (180–200 °C) for an additional 10–15 minutes.

RECIPES

SCALLOPED GYROS FRENCH FRY CASSEROLE

INGREDIENTS FOR 4 SERVINGS

2 ¼ pounds (1 kg) gyros meat cut into strips

2 ¼ pound (1 kg) french fries

2 medium onions

1 ¾ cups (400 ml) whipped cream

½ bunch kitchen herbs (thyme, rosemary, basil etc.)

12 slices cheese (butter cheese)

4 tbsp oil, for browning

PREPARATION

✪ Dice the onions into small cubes and sear together with the gyros in a bit of oil. Finely chop the kitchen herbs, mix in the whipped cream, add to the gyros and briefly bring to a boil. Evenly spread the mixture into a casserole dish.

✪ Shape the french fries as desired, wash, dry and after dripping some oil on top blanch about 20 minutes at 390°F (200°C). Spread the french fries over the gyros and sprinkle with half of the butter cheese that has been torn into small pieces. Put the casserole into the oven at 390°F (200 C). As soon as the cheese melts, sprinkle the rest of the cheese onto the casserole and bake the whole thing for another 15–20 minutes.

PITA BREAD WITH FRENCH FRIES

INGREDIENTS FOR 4 SERVINGS

1 pita bread

1 pound (500 g) french fries

1/2 cucumber

7 ounces (200 g) tzatziki

7 ounces (200 g) feta cheese

1/4 cup (50 g) field salad

paprika powder

salt

PREPARATION

✪ Shape the french fries as desired, wash, dry and deep-fry. Then season to taste with salt and paprika powder.

✪ Wash and dry the field salad. Slice the cucumber into thin slices, dice the feta cheese.

✪ Crisp up the pita bread in the oven for approx. 2–3 minutes at 250°F (120°C). Then quarter it and cut open pockets starting at the tip. Spread tzatziki on the bread and cover with cucumbers. Next, place the field salad and french fries into the pockets and sprinkle with feta cheese.

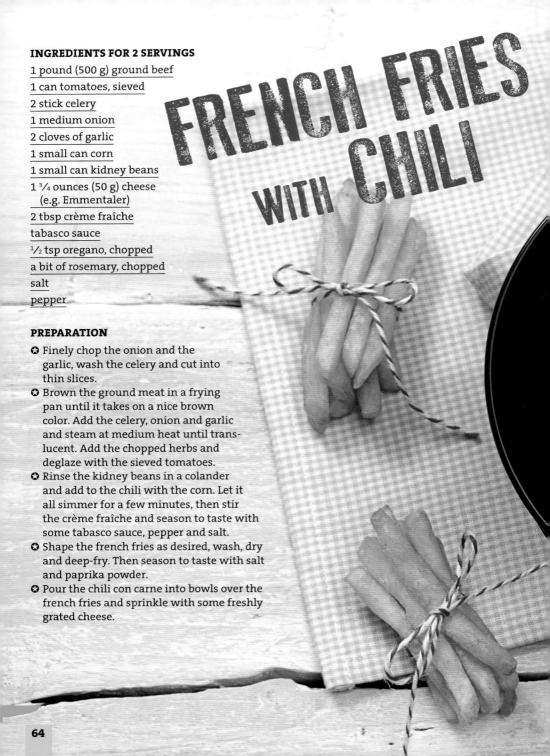

INGREDIENTS FOR 2 SERVINGS

1 pound (500 g) ground beef

1 can tomatoes, sieved

2 stick celery

1 medium onion

2 cloves of garlic

1 small can corn

1 small can kidney beans

1 ³/₄ ounces (50 g) cheese
(e.g. Emmentaler)

2 tbsp crème fraîche

tabasco sauce

¹/₂ tsp oregano, chopped

a bit of rosemary, chopped

salt

pepper

FRENCH FRIES WITH CHILI

PREPARATION

✪ Finely chop the onion and the garlic, wash the celery and cut into thin slices.

✪ Brown the ground meat in a frying pan until it takes on a nice brown color. Add the celery, onion and garlic and steam at medium heat until translucent. Add the chopped herbs and deglaze with the sieved tomatoes.

✪ Rinse the kidney beans in a colander and add to the chili with the corn. Let it all simmer for a few minutes, then stir the crème fraîche and season to taste with some tabasco sauce, pepper and salt.

✪ Shape the french fries as desired, wash, dry and deep-fry. Then season to taste with salt and paprika powder.

✪ Pour the chili con carne into bowls over the french fries and sprinkle with some freshly grated cheese.

FRENCH FRY BURGER

INGREDIENTS FOR 2 SERVINGS

2 sesame hamburger buns
$\frac{1}{2}$ pound (250 g) french fries
4 slices of cheese (e.g. cheddar)
hot dog sauce
fried onions

PREPARATION

✪ Shape the french fries as desired, wash, dry and deep-fry. Then season to taste with salt and paprika powder.

✪ Cut open the hamburger buns. Put one slice of cheese on each half and place in the oven for a few minutes at approx. 250°F (120°C) until the cheese melts.

✪ Spread plenty of hot dog sauce onto the hamburger buns, cover with french fries, sprinkle with the fried onions and serve immediately.

HOT DOG SAUCE

INGREDIENTS

2 large onions
4 $\frac{1}{4}$ ounces (125 ml) ketchup
2 tsp white wine vinegar
2 tbsp brown sugar
1 pinch of salt
some pepper
a bit of cayenne pepper or chili powder

PREPARATION

✪ Let the onion rings, ketchup, vinegar and spices simmer in a covered pot for at least 15 minutes until the onions are very soft.

OPEN SESAME ...

INGREDIENTS FOR 2 SERVINGS

1 pound (500 g) potatoes, floury
1 cup (150 g) sesame seed
1 egg
some flour

PREPARATION

✪ Peel the potatoes, wash and first cut into finger thick slices, then into sticks.
✪ Roll the potato sticks in flour so they are covered uniformly on all sides. Whisk the egg in a plate and coat the floured potato sticks with it. Then roll the potato sticks in the sesame seeds.
✪ Place the breaded french fries on a baking sheet and bake until yellow gold for approx. 15–20 minutes at approx. 390°F (200°C).

STRAW POTATOES

INGREDIENTS FOR 4 SERVINGS

4 large potatoes

paprika, sweet

salt

pepper

PREPARATION

- Peel the potatoes, wash, cut into very thin strips or cut julienne and pat dry with a towel.
- Deep-fry the potato strips a portion at a time for 4 minutes each at approx. 350°F (175°C). Lift out the "straw" with a skimmer and let it drip dry on paper towels. Season with salt, pepper and paprika powder and serve hot.

BELGIAN FRENCH FRIES
WITH THYME & PARMESAN

INGREDIENTS
FOR 2 SERVINGS

1 pound (500 g) potatoes, floury

3 tbsp olive oil

1 tsp thyme

2 tbsp parmesan

salt

pepper

PREPARATION

✪ Shape the french fries as desired, wash, dry and place in a bowl. Add the olive oil, the freshly chopped thyme and the freshly ground parmesan and mix thoroughly until the potato sticks are covered uniformly on all sides.

✪ Preheat the oven to 355°F (180°C). Spread the french fries evenly on a parchment covered baking sheet, salt, pepper and bake for 20 minutes. Carefully loosen the french fries from the parchment paper with a spatula, distribute onto plates and serve hot.

VEGETABLES

No matter how much we love french fries, of course, it's not just potatoes that can be deep fried with great success. Particularly suited are vegetable varieties that are rich in starch or solid, like carrots, sweet potatoes or parsnips, but also eggplants and zucchini. Even fish, meat, cheese or baked goods taste scrumptious deep fried. Types that are too soft and items for deep frying that have very few carbohydrates should be protected with a coating or a layer of batter from drying out or falling apart.

SWEET POTATO FRENCH FRIES

INGREDIENTS FOR 4 SERVINGS

6 sweet potatoes

salt

olive oil

PREPARATION

✪ Peel the sweet potatoes and cut into finger thick slices, next, split them into about finger thick sticks. Place the sweet potato french fries into a bowl with some olive oil and mix well.

✪ Place the french fry sticks onto a parchment covered baking sheet and bake at 390-410°F (200–210°C) for approx. 20 minutes. Check occasionally to make sure the sticks aren't burning.

✪ Sprinkle the baked sweet potato sticks with some coarse salt and serve hot with the sweet potato royale dip *(recipe see page 55)*.

ZUCCHINI FRENCH FRIES

INGREDIENTS FOR 4 SERVINGS

2 large zucchini

2 small cloves of garlic

1 tbsp oregano, freshly chopped

4 tbsp olive oil

1 tsp salt

PREPARATION

- Wash the zucchini thoroughly, cut in half and then into finger thick strips. Crush the clove of garlic and put it in a bowl with zucchini sticks, the olive oil, the freshly chopped oregano and the salt. Mix well.
- Preheat the oven to 320°F (160°C). Place the zucchini strips onto a parchment covered baking sheet and bake for about 15 minutes.

CELERY FRENCH FRIES

INGREDIENTS FOR 2 SERVINGS

1 pound (500 g) celery root

5 tbsp flour

75 g bread crumbs

2 eggs

1 cup (250 ml) oil

pepper

salt

PREPARATION

- Clean the celery, peel and cut into finger thick slices, then cut them into finger thick sticks. Blanch the celery french fries in boiling salt water for about 2 minutes, lift out with a skimmer, shock with cold water and let it drip dry well.
- Distribute the flour, whisked eggs and bread crumbs into separate deep plates. Dry the celery sticks thoroughly once more with a kitchen towel.
- A serving at a time turn the celery french fries first in flour, then in egg and then in the bread crumbs so they are uniformly breaded on all sides.
- Deep-fry the breaded celery french fries in approx. 350°F (175°C) hot oil for about 3 minutes until a golden yellow. Let them briefly dry on paper towels and serve hot with Zoe's Cajun Sauce *(recipe see page 53)*.

SWEET FRENCH FRIES

INGREDIENTS FOR 6 SERVINGS

10 slices bread for toasting
2 ¼ cups (250) g strawberries
5 ripe apricots
2 cups (400 g) cream quark
2 tbsp liquid honey
2–3 tbsp sugar
1 pinch of cinnamon

PREPARATION

✪ Cut the crust off two opposite edges of the bread. Then cut the slices into five uniform strips each so that there remains crust at the top and bottom edges. Spread the strips on a parchment covered baking sheet. Mix the cinnamon with the sugar and distribute among the spread out strips.

✪ Preheat the oven to 390°F (200°C) and bake the toast strips to a golden brown on the second rail from the bottom for about 15–18 minutes until the sugar caramelizes.

✪ Mix the cream quark with the honey. Wash and clean the strawberries and wash and pit the apricots. Cut the fruit into small cubes and lift under the honey quark.

✪ Remove the toasted french fries from the oven, let them cool and serve with the fruit quark.

MARDI GRAS FRENCH FRIES WITH DRIED FRUIT

INGREDIENTS FOR 4 SERVINGS

2 cups (500 g) flour	1 pinch of salt
½ cups (100 g) sugar	sugar
4 ½ ounces (125 g butter	cinnamon
2 eggs	2 cups (500 ml) deep-frying oil
some milk	13 ounces (375 g) mixed fruit
1 packet backing powder	1 cinnamon stick
some lemon peel	¼ cup (50 g) sugar

PREPARATION

✪ Whip the room temperature butter with the sugar, eggs and lemon peels for a few minutes with a hand mixer until foamy. Slowly add the flour and paking powder. Add enough milk to create a smooth dough.

✪ Knead the dough by hand on a countertop until it is a smooth dough. Then roll into an approx. ½ cm thick sheet. Shape into french fries with a knife or a dough wheel.

✪ Deep-fry the Mardi Gras french fries floating in small servings in the hot fat. Lift out with a skimmer and turn in sugar and cinnamon.

✪ For the dried fruit wash the fruit the previous evening, peel if necessary, cut into small pieces and soak in ½ liter water. The next day add the cinnamon stick, some lemon peel and the sugar and slowly cook until soft at a medium temperature.